HELEN EDMUNDSON

Helen Edmundson's first play, *Flying*, was presented at the National Theatre Studio in 1990. She first came to notice in 1992 with her adaptation of *Anna Karenina* for Shared Experience, for whom she also adapted *The Mill on the Floss* in 1994. Both won awards – the TMA and the Time Out Awards respectively – and both productions were twice revived and extensively toured.

The Clearing was first staged at The Bush Theatre in 1993, winning John Whiting and Time Out Awards, and was revived and toured by Shared Experience, who also staged her adaptation of *War and Peace* at the National Theatre in 1996 and *Gone to Earth* on tour in 2004. *Mother Teresa is Dead* was premiered at the Royal Court Theatre in 2002. *Coram Boy* premiered at the National Theatre London to critical acclaim in 2005, and received a Time Out Award. Helen Edmundson lives in West London with her actor husband and their two children.

D1423792

Helen Edmundson

ORESTES
Blood and Light

Based on Euripides

NICK HERN BOOKS
London

www.nickhernbooks.co.uk

A Nick Hern Book

This adaptation of *Orestes* first published in Great Britain
as a paperback original in 2006 by Nick Hern Books Limited,
14 Larden Road, London W3 7ST

Orestes copyright © 2005 Helen Edmundson

Helen Edmundson has asserted her right to be identified
as the adapter of this work

Cover image design: Eureka Designs for Shared Experience
Cover design by Ned Hoste, 2H

Typeset by Country Setting, Kingsdown, Kent CT14 8ES
Printed in Great Britain by Biddles Ltd, King's Lynn, Norfolk

A CIP catalogue record for this book is available from
the British Library

ISBN-13   978 1 85459 894 3
ISBN-10   1 85459 894 5

This version of *Orestes* was first performed by Shared
Experience Theatre Company at the Yvonne Arnaud Theatre,
Guildford, on 14 September 2006; and subsequently at Dublin
Theatre Festival; Warwick Arts Centre; The Lowry, Salford;
Liverpool Playhouse; Oxford Playhouse; and Tricycle Theatre,
London. The cast was as follows:

MENELAOS	Tim Chipping
TYNDAREOS	Jeffery Kissoon
ELECTRA	Mairead McKinley
HELEN	Clara Onyemere
SLAVE	Claire Prempeh
ORESTES	Alex Robertson

Director   Nancy Meckler
Designer   Niki Turner
Lighting Designer   Peter Harrison
Composer   Peter Salem
Company Movement   Liz Ranken

Foreword

When Nancy Meckler first gave me Euripides' version of
Orestes to read, I was puzzled by it. It is structurally flawed
and tonally inconsistent. Although classed as a tragedy, its
ending, in which a god descends and puts everything to rights,
is a happy, if hollow, one. For these reasons it is rarely performed
and often over-looked in discussions of his work, but the ideas
contained within it are fascinating. The more we talked, the
more I understood why Nancy was drawn to it. I understood
the sad and frightening number of ways in which it is relevant
to the current state of the world. When I began writing I was
thinking as much about George Bush disregarding the views
of the UN, and Tony Blair praying to God for guidance before
invading Iraq, as I was about suicide bombers and religious
extremists. I was thinking as much about honour killings
amongst religious communities as about the loss of faith in
the integrity of government and the impartiality of law.

As I wrote, I found the story allowed me to go even further.
The way the characters use religion to justify their actions
opened up into questions about the very nature of faith and the
complex relationship between Man and his Gods, whilst
Electra's damaged, desperate heart speaks volumes about the
personal, deep-rooted pain that underlies so many acts of
violence, both on small and large scales.

I confess I have played fast and loose with the conventions of
Greek theatre and with Euripides' version of the story. I have
abandoned the Chorus (who is not active or influential in the
Euripides) in favour of the more subtle witness of the Slave.
I have cut the character of Pylades to allow Electra her full
role in the story and to allow myself to explore the extremities
of her relationship with her brother. I have given Helen an
intelligent, probing mind and allowed her and Klytemnestra
some defence. I have chosen not to emulate the verse structure
and metres of Euripides' text, but to try to create a rhythmic,
heightened language of my own.

In short, I have followed my instincts. I have kept what is useful to me and lost what is not in the hope of creating a drama which can speak freely, freshly and vitally to audiences today.

Helen Edmundson

ORESTES

Characters

ELECTRA
ORESTES
HELEN
SLAVE
MENELAOS
TYNDAREOS
SOLDIERS
ATTENDANTS

*A forward slash (/) in the dialogue indicates that the next
character begins speaking at that point. If the forward slash
appears at the end of a character's line of dialogue, it
indicates that the character continues their next line of
dialogue without a break.*

*This text went to press before the end of rehearsals so may
differ slightly from the play as performed.*

In Klytemnestra's bedroom in Agamemnon's palace. It is an ostentatious room, full of clothes and pairs of shoes, full of the gold-plated trappings of wealth.

ELECTRA *is sitting at the dressing table. She is wearing one of her mother's dresses over the top of her own clothes.*

ORESTES *is on the bed, asleep.*

ELECTRA. Sometimes she would let me stay while she undressed. Sometimes she would send the servants away and she would sit here while I brushed her hair. My mother. She would let me open jars and bottles, sniff and touch, she would let me uncover close things from drawers, treasures, and tell me where they came from. Tell me stories of a life before. Sometimes she would hold out her hands for me and I would rub them with oil, taking the rings off, one by one, feeling the deep lines on her knuckles, shifting her skin, gently, over veins and bone.

I wanted to climb back inside her, always, and settle down behind her heart.

The best day . . . the best day was when my father came home triumphant in wine and pride and said he had betrothed me to a prince, though I was only six years old, Prince Kastor of Sparta, a demigod, a god to be. That day I was the centre of my mother's eye. She dressed me as a princess, put colour on my lips and cheeks, a golden crown upon my head. And my father lifted me up on his shoulders, a horse for a virgin-bride, and staggered me around the room, cornering and swaying, laughing loud while my mother played the easy, adoring people.

And that night I crawled into bed beside my mother, that bed, and when my father came he didn't tip me out but let me stay. And I crept down and down, burrowing between them, smelling in the mattress and the sheets all their nights of passion and sweat, good dreams and bad, our warmth all mingling together.

He was naked when she killed him. Naked in his bath, his home bath, his safe bath. Naked. His muscles releasing their memories of battle and rough seas. They netted him – my mother and her lover Aigisthos – they caught him round with cord, with rope. He stood, too late. He struggled, twisted, they brought him down, crashing to his knees, arms pressed against his sides like giant, folded wings. He moaned, roared, spat, they swung the axe and split his skull, they swung again, they hacked his chest until it cracked, they axed and axed until his moving, twitching stopped and blood lapped the sides of the bath with a steady, slowing rhythm. My father.

Someone had to see. It was right that it should be me. Right for my father, right for him – (*She indicates the sleeping* ORESTES.) so that I could tell him, perfectly, what she had done. I didn't need to fable it, tell how she danced and sang while he lay dying, wound garlands through her hair. I could tell him how she sagged and felt for the floor, vomiting and shaking. I could tell him how Aigisthos stood so still and Time gaped, gasped. Time gasped.

If I hadn't seen it, we might have balked at what we had to do. My brother and I. Orestes.

Beyond the doors, footsteps and noises are heard.
ELECTRA *springs up, terrified.*

No. No. Who's there? It isn't time yet. Leave us alone. Let my brother sleep. Let us have our last night. Who's there?

The doors open and HELEN *enters with* SOLDIERS *in attendance. Also with her is a female* SLAVE *who is carrying* HELEN's *baby daughter,* HERMIONE.

ELECTRA *stares in disbelief.* HELEN *stands still and takes in the scene.*

HELEN. Do you recognise me?

ELECTRA. Yes.

HELEN. Speak my name.

ELECTRA. Helen. You are Helen, if you are real.

HELEN. I haven't changed so much. Unlike you, Electra. You were a child when I left.

ELECTRA. You're back.

HELEN. Sixteen years.

ELECTRA. You're back.

HELEN. Yes. I'm back.

ELECTRA. My uncle? Is he with you?

HELEN. 'Uncle' Menelaos. He'll be here. Soon. He sent me on ahead under cover of darkness, to slip unseen through the city gates. He feared the people would be baying for my blood, poor souls who lost their sons to the war. But the people have scented fresh blood now.

(*To* SOLDIERS.) Bring more light in here.

(*Looking at* ORESTES.) Is this your brother?

ELECTRA. Yes. It is Orestes.

HELEN. Wake him up.

ELECTRA. No. Please. No. He hasn't slept for six days and nights. He hasn't closed his eyes.

HELEN. Since he murdered his mother? Since he murdered my sister?

ELECTRA. We both did it. I did it too. Apollo told us to.

HELEN *moves further into the room, seeing things more clearly in the new light.*

HELEN. This room. A mausoleum. It smells of her. (*She picks up a hairbrush from the dressing table.*) Is this her hair?

ELECTRA. Yes.

HELEN. It was always stronger than mine, though it never shone so well. Is this where she died?

ELECTRA. No.

HELEN. Where then? Where did she die? My sister?

ELECTRA. In the hills outside the city. After they killed my
    father – she and Aigisthos – they wanted me gone. They
    married me to a farmer, a peasant, a man much older than
    myself, so that any son I should chance to have would be
    too low to set himself against them. But Orestes came. Back
    from long years away. He found me, knew me. Our hands
    locked together. He told me what Apollo had decreed and so
    we lured them to us and we killed them. And then we came
    home.

    Now the people are angry with us. They call us the matricides.
    By day they press around the palace walls. They leave the
    rotting carcasses of dogs beneath the windows. They have
    nailed shut the wells and taken the wood so that we have
    no warmth. In the assembly, in our absence, we have been
    tried and condemned. Tomorrow they decide how we should
    die – by public execution, or abandoned to the mob.
    Tomorrow is the last day.

    We gave her a decent burial. We passed her through
    cleansing fire. There is a tomb, you will see, a proper place
    where prayers can be said and offerings can be made.

    We did what Apollo asked of us. We are in his hands. We
    commend ourselves to our God.

HELEN. Pretty dress, Electra. Was it one of hers?

    (*To* SOLDIERS.) Open up another wing of the palace. Away
    from here. Go out and find food, water, wood. If anyone
    should challenge you, say you come in Menelaos' name.
    Make somewhere safe and clean for myself and my
    daughter and my husband.

    HELEN *starts to go.*

ELECTRA. Helen?

    Tomorrow is the last day.

HELEN. Yes.

ELECTRA. If you find water . . . if you could spare some for Orestes. He is ill. He is hot, feverish. A little food perhaps?

HELEN *turns to go again.*

Helen. Talk to Menelaos. Please. We know our lives are gone, but ask him, please . . . not the mob. We are Agamemnon's children. We shouldn't die like that. Please ask him that.

HELEN *comes to stand close to her.*

HELEN. Are you still a virgin?

ELECTRA. Yes. My husband was a good man. He had no wish to shame me.

HELEN. Is that what he told you?

You are unlovable, Electra. And unloved. It happens sometimes; a child is born who cannot be loved.

The third of three girls, what possible use could you be? You were a prelude to Orestes; a mistake, a slip.

Your mother knew it and you knew it too. You are a warren of need, more holes than self. If I tried to look for you, where would I find you? Here? Here? There is nothing to be found.

What a chance this was for you, what an opportunity to punish her for what she didn't do, for all the smiles you didn't get, each kiss that never met your lips, the long appalling nightmare of her indifference.

ELECTRA. My mother loved me.

HELEN. The only affection you ever knew was from your sister, Iphegenia, who cared for you from pity, nothing more. Your beautiful, glorious sister who your father took away and slew, who he tricked from the safety of your mother's arms and slaughtered in the full glare of the sun, all the knowledge of her own death banging in her heart and head – /

ELECTRA. Because of you! /

HELEN. Knowing that he cared more for a fair wind than he did for her.

ELECTRA. A fair wind to take him after you. So they could all go running after you, / because you couldn't stay in your own bed.

HELEN. Why didn't you kill your father? Your murderous, treacherous father?

ELECTRA. My father? Don't speak about my father. You are not even worthy to / speak his name.

HELEN. Agamemnon. The great and good. He took your mother first by force, did you know that? She had a husband before he found her. He killed him, dashed out the brains of the child that she had born. Did they tell you that? And she submitted. She submitted and submitted every day, stretched her heart to cover him but it was too much. Iphegenia was too much.

ELECTRA. You talk as though you had no part in it. She was sacrificed for you.

HELEN. Where was your anger then, Electra? Or did you smile? Smile at the acid thrill of a sister's death, a mother's grief?

ELECTRA. No.

HELEN. She needed you, did she? After that? Kept you with her through the nights, you washed her face, fed her morsels, kept her alive, my child, my child, and then she found her lover and you were nothing – /

ELECTRA. No.

HELEN. And you were back in the corner. Back in the dark.

ELECTRA. You are just the same as her. Both of you the same. Both of you are whores.

HELEN. Yes. Yes, yes. Ring your virginity like a leper's bell. What do you know of what we do? What do you know of a woman's heart? You will never feel the weight of a man, you will never be kissed between your legs, no great moment of ecstasy will ever blur the lines of your pristine vision.

Do not judge me.

What do you know of any of it? Bargains made in silence beneath the sheets, sealed with babies, bodies, a hundred different ways to pay. Do not judge me.

Why did I do it? Why did I go? Because I am a bitch on heat? Because Menelaos was not man enough to keep me? Because Paris was not made to be resisted, who shall we blame? Leda, my mother? Zeus, my father, for covering her with his wings and giving me this face, this power, this light to draw men on? Who shall we blame? Let's unpick the earth like a tapestry until there is nothing left.

Electra. Electra. You are lying to me or you are lying to yourself. Apollo told you to do it. Did he so?

ELECTRA. Yes.

HELEN. The Gods speak and you obey.

ELECTRA. Yes.

HELEN. There is a meeting place between Gods and man – I should know, it is tangible in me – a battle between blood and light, and it is in that place that all is decided and actions are taken and life is lived.

ELECTRA. I don't understand what you're saying.

HELEN. I think you do.

ORESTES *has awoken and cries out.*

ORESTES. Apollo. My Lord God, help me.

ELECTRA. Orestes?

ORESTES. Away. Stay away from me. You are not my mother.

He is terrified.

ELECTRA. Orestes.

ORESTES. Away.

HELEN. He thinks you are her.

ELECTRA. He has been like this since . . .

ORESTES. Apollo. Apollo, where are you now? She's here. She's here. Help me, protect me. Where is the horn-sprung bow you promised me?

ELECTRA. Orestes, stop.

ORESTES (*to* HELEN). You are not my mother. You are not her. She is dead. I killed her with these hands. Get away from me. There is nothing for you here. You cannot take my soul, my soul is gone.

He sees the SLAVE *with the baby.*

Oh, no. Oh, no. She tore her dress. She showed me her breast. Would you bring me death where I gave you life? Would you bring me death where I gave you life? Would you bring me death where I gave you life? Strike me twice, a woman and a mother. Kill me twice, my baby. No.You are not my mother. You are not my mother.

ELECTRA. Orestes, no. Look at me. I am Electra. Electra. I am Electra.

ORESTES. Electra?

He stops still. He sinks down and lets out a terrible, long moan.

Oh –

He begins to weep. ELECTRA *puts her arms around him.*

HELEN. I pity him. He feels the guilt for you both.

HELEN *leaves.*

ELECTRA. Orestes, don't. My sweet brother, don't. I'm here. I'm here. I'm here with you forever, in life and death. Don't. Don't cry.

ORESTES. I'm so afraid.

ELECTRA. I know. And I am too.

ORESTES. She came again.

ELECTRA. She wasn't here.

ORESTES. Electra, listen to me. Listen. Listen, while my head is my own. My eyes are my own now, my tongue. Listen to me: we should not have done it.

ELECTRA. Hush. Hush now.

ORESTES. We should not have done it. It is unforgivable. It is against nature, against the world, against life. I had a life. You had a life. There is nothing left now.

ELECTRA. Hush. You are ill. You are feverish.

ORESTES. He would not have wanted us to do it.

ELECTRA. Who?

ORESTES. Our father.

ELECTRA. No.

ORESTES. He would have begged us not to do it.

ELECTRA. No. You're wrong.

ORESTES. Not for her sake but for our own. He would have begged us not to cast aside our own humanity, because without it there is nothing.

ELECTRA. Then he would have been thinking of us. But it was him we had to think of. We had to do what was right for him.

ORESTES. It was right but it was not good.

She was our mother.

ELECTRA. Don't think that I don't feel it as you feel it. It was I who put the sword into your hand.

ORESTES. And I who struck her down.

Our mother.

ELECTRA. We did not begin this. Of course . . . of course it would have been better if we had never had to do it, if none of this had ever happened, but it did. We had to act for him. We had to bring him peace.

Where would we be now if we hadn't done it? How could we have lived? Knowing that he was in perpetual darkness and there was no one else to set him free?

ORESTES. It was Apollo's will.

ELECTRA. Yes. Yes. It was Apollo's will.

Orestes, my Orestes, He said you would suffer. He told you that. Do you remember?

ORESTES. Yes. It is all as he said it would be. All of it. Forgive me. Please forgive me.

ELECTRA. Hush now. Quiet now. Quiet now. Tomorrow it will all be over. Tomorrow we will be released and it will all be over. Look at me. Tomorrow we will go to Apollo. We will be rocked in Apollo's arms in a place where there is only gentleness and kindness, where we will have no troubles, no worries, no weight, where our desires will be fulfilled before they are conceived, where we will be all satisfaction.

The SLAVE *has begun to sing to the baby, a haunting lullaby in her own language.*

Orestes, my brother, my only brother. You were gone from me for so long, taken away from me. Your skin smells of islands where I have never been, your hands are larger than mine, your muscles are harder, stronger than mine and yet we are the same. You are me. You are my insides. And I am yours. We are bound together in this and all things. Orestes, my brother, sleep now. Lie down. Sleep. Sleep beside me, your sister. Feel my fingers in amongst your hair. Sleep now. Hearts together. My own heart. Sleep.

The SLAVE *stops singing and asks suddenly –*

SLAVE. Is this a good country they have brought me to? Is this a good country they have brought me to?

ELECTRA *closes her eyes and she and* ORESTES *sleep.*

The SLAVE *leaves. Darkness descends. After a few moments, a man enters, almost silently. It is* MENELAOS. *He waits for his eyes to adjust to the light. He sees the*

sleeping pair. He sits down, close by and watches them.
Dawn breaks.

ORESTES *awakens. He sees* MENELAOS, *but does not*
know who he is.

ORESTES. Is that the sun?

Is it time?

We have slept too long.

We were tired.

He struggles to sit up.

MENELAOS. Let me help you.

ORESTES. No. I don't need help. I feel better today.

Have you come for us?

Is it only you? One man to take us to our death. They send
one man for the children of a king. Is that arrogance, or
respect?

He coughs. MENELAOS *hands him a bottle of water.*

MENELAOS. Here.

ORESTES *drinks.*

ORESTES. Thank you.

MENELAOS. Finish it.

ORESTES. No. No. She needs some too.

He watches ELECTRA.

My sister.

As a child she must have looked like this. I wish I could
remember. When my father went to war they sent me away
so that I would be safe. Their infant son. Their precious boy.
But there is safe and safe. I wish I could have stayed. I wish
I could have played with her, fought with her, been bored
with her. I wish we could have slept, just once, with our
heads on our mother's lap. Things might have been different
then.

Do you think things would have been different? Is it possible for one small fact to change everything?

MENELAOS. I don't know.

ORESTES. I don't know.

If I could die twice today and save her, I would.

MENELAOS. You have your father's too-tender heart, Orestes.

ORESTES. Did you know my father?

MENELAOS. I knew your father well.

ORESTES. Then you are luckier than I am.

Did you fight beside him?

MENELAOS. Many times. A General of generals. A King of kings.

ORESTES. You loved him.

MENELAOS. Yes.

ORESTES. Then you must grieve for him as I do.

MENELAOS. More, perhaps, than anyone, I grieve for him. Orestes, I am not who you think I am. I have not come to take you to your death. I am your uncle – Menelaos. I am Agamemnon's brother. Menelaos.

Forgive me. Please. I needed to see you, to watch you. I know so little of you. The only thing I do know, I wish with all my heart I didn't.

ORESTES. Menelaos?

MENELAOS. Yes. It is the truth.

ORESTES. Menelaos. Uncle. My father's brother. My blood.

ORESTES *rushes towards him but almost collapses.*

MENELAOS (*helping him*). You are ill. Here. Here.

ORESTES. No. I am better. I am better today.

MENELAOS. Helen told me you were ranting, feverish.

ORESTES. Helen?

MENELAOS. Helen is with me. And our baby daughter too.
Hermione. Our hope. I have brought them home.

ORESTES. Apollo has brought you back to me.

MENELAOS. Back from sixteen years of war and wandering.
The last six years our ship was lost upon the seas, driven
from one strange coast to another. I knew my brother would
reach home before me. It was what sustained me – the
thought of his welcome here in the city, his sweet reunion
with his wife, with Klytemnestra, in this room, in that very
bed, I pictured it. I pictured his children gathered around
him as he stood on the balcony and addressed the people,
his figurehead chest swelling with pride as he described to
them our victories.

Then, one day, we came to a country, a thriving place,
where they told me stories of my brother's death, stories so
particular in detail that they could not be dismissed, of how
he died in his bath, killed by his own wife's hand.

ORESTES. True. All true.

MENELAOS. I wept then. I wept and raved against the Gods. I
raised a mound for him, a cenotaph. With my own hands I
struck his name into the stone.

ORESTES. Thank you. Thank you.

MENELAOS. Then yesterday, when we, at last, had reached
the coast, before I had set foot on land they called across to
me from the quay, Klytemnestra is dead, killed by her
children, the matricides.

ORESTES. And now we in turn will die. Today the assembly
meet to decide our death.

MENELAOS. Orestes. Why did you stay? You should have
crossed the border. Sought sanctuary.

ORESTES. I was too weak to run. This grief. This guilt. If it
were not for Electra I would be dead already.

I see her, Menelaos. When my eyes are open, when my eyes are closed. When the sun is up. When the moon is out. I see her. Last night . . . last night she was as real to me as you are now.

This is not something to be run from.

MENELAOS. I understand.

ORESTES. It is a part of me now. (*Indicating* ELECTRA.) A part of us.

MENELAOS. Yes.

ORESTES. I, like you, have just returned from years away, to be where I should be, ruling in this palace as my father ruled. It is the only fate I want. The fate I have cherished, prepared for since I first become aware of who I am.

MENELAOS. Yes.

ORESTES. And now it can happen. Because you are here. You have come and everything has changed. You will help us, Uncle?

MENELAOS. Yes. Of course I will help you.

ORESTES. My father was your true brother. He went to war for you, protected you and now you protect me. You save me. And Electra too.

MENELAOS. Yes.

ORESTES. How right this is. How good and right this is. Electra. Electra. Wake up. Look, and try to believe what you see.

She opens her eyes and sits up.

It is Menelaos. It is our uncle.

ELECTRA. Uncle? Uncle.

She falls at MENELAOS' *feet and begins to weep.*

MENELAOS. Don't. Don't cry, Electra.

ELECTRA. How can I not cry? You are so like my father. They hurt him, Uncle.

MENELAOS. I know.

ELECTRA. They trapped him. He didn't stand a chance.

MENELAOS. If only I had been here. They would not have touched him then.

ELECTRA. They buried him with nothing. No offerings, no sacrifice.

MENELAOS. It is cruel beyond belief.

ELECTRA. They tipped his blood away like dirty water. I saw them carry out the bath. They tipped away his blood into a rancid stream.

MENELAOS. Hush now. There is no need to speak of this.

He raises her to her feet.

I am back. No more weeping.

ORESTES. I had no hope before you came, but now I know we will not die today.

Footsteps are heard outside the doors. TYNDAREOS' *voice rings out.*

TYNDAREOS (*off*). Where is he? Search.

ORESTES. They're coming.

MENELAOS. I know that voice. My father-in-law –
Tyndareos.

ELECTRA. Grandfather.

ORESTES. Our grandfather?

ELECTRA. Why does he come now?

MENELAOS. Because I am here. He must have heard I have returned. And Helen too.

ELECTRA (*to* ORESTES). Move back into the shadows. He doesn't need to see you.

ORESTES. No. I will face him. I must face him. I am strong enough for anything today.

The doors are thrust open and TYNDAREOS *enters with* ATTENDANTS. *He stares at* MENELAOS.

TYNDAREOS. So it's true then.

MENELAOS. I am glad to see you again, Tyndareos, after all these years.

TYNDAREOS. I would be glad to see you anywhere, Menelaos, but not here.

MENELAOS. Where else would I go? Agamemnon's Palace. The seat of my Fathers.

TYNDAREOS. This place is contaminated now, and will be so until those two are dead. Then it can be cleansed and prayers can be said. Then and only then will it be fit to rule from.

MENELAOS. I wanted to see my brother's children. To listen to them. You have always defended a man's right to have his say.

TYNDAREOS. They have no rights. Murderers have no rights.

MENELAOS. Surely every man has rights.

ORESTES. Grandfather?

TYNDAREOS. Is it true that she is here? My so-called daughter, Helen?

MENELAOS. Yes. I have brought her home. And our child too.

TYNDAREOS. Your child, you say?

MENELAOS. A baby daughter, born at sea.

TYNDAREOS. You think that will keep her with you? Even a branded beast will stray, Menelaos.

MENELAOS. We are a family now. Let me call them to you.

TYNDAREOS. No. I have not come here for reconciliations. I have come for one reason alone, to warn you not to try to stand between these two and their certain fate.

MENELAOS. To 'warn me'?

ORESTES. Grandfather?

TYNDAREOS. Do not call me so. I am no kin of yours. Look
at you – a shambling criminal, more dead than alive, dried
blood under your fingernails, you have no claim on me. I
thank the Gods I never grew to love you. So much the easier
now for me to turn my back on you.

MENELAOS. Don't speak so harshly, Tyndareos. He is your
kin. He is your kin and mine too. We help him and we
honour him.

TYNDAREOS. Not when he has broken the law.

MENELAOS. I hold to a greater law.

TYNDAREOS. Your wandering has left you soft, Menelaos.

MENELAOS. And your age has left you hard.

TYNDAREOS. Things have changed here since you left. We
have sharpened the edges of our democracy.

MENELAOS. And put an end to mercy, it would seem.

TYNDAREOS. Mercy? There is no place for mercy here.
What mercy did he show his mother?

MENELAOS. As much, perhaps, as I would have shown, had I
arrived here first.

TYNDAREOS. You would not have been so rash, Menelaos,
and you know it.

I don't excuse my daughter, Klytemnestra, for what she did,
but she was, after all, a woman, and fractured with passion
like all her kind. But when he heard of Agamemnon's death
he should have stuck to the law, our law, hard-won,
ordained by the Gods. Our laws are there to stop the chain
of death on death. Any man with blood on his hands should
be banished, outcast, not seen or spoken to. That is what he
should have called for. That would have been fit punishment
for her, clean punishment for her. Then he would have won
respect, admiration for his wisdom, his his circumspection.
But no. He judged her beyond the law, he sank beneath her
level and so he threatens the whole of civilisation.

We are not animals. Do you understand me? We are not animals. You make me sick to look at you. I heard she bared her breast, begged you for mercy and yet still you struck her – the body which gave you life. I have wept to think of it. I am not ashamed to say that. I try to sleep at night and my mind flinches, my body fits at the image of her face, her fear, the whites of her eyes, her hand raised against the blade.

The Gods hate you, Orestes. Your blasted wits are proof of that. If you help him, Menelaos, you defy the Gods and you defy the law. Leave him. Let the people stone him to death and then it will be done with.

ORESTES. Grandfather – for you are still my grandfather, the father of my mother and the man I must respect, my father gone, above all others. I have long pictured the moment of our meeting; the chance to be able to touch you, talk with you, learn from you. I had hoped to undo, with one embrace, all the years of separation and unknowingness. I had hoped that the cord, from your centre to mine, would pull us tight together.

TYNDAREOS. You severed that cord.

ORESTES. The thought that I have caused you pain is almost impossible for me to bear, and yet I must risk hurting you further now for I cannot let you go without begging you to listen to what I have to say and asking that you try to understand me.

Do you think this was easy for me? An easy decision – to kill my mother? You think my wits are shaken now with guilt, but they were shaken first by the long, tortured days which followed when I learnt what she had done. Long days of questioning and turmoil. I was so far away, separate, no family to ask advice of – Menelaos, you. I forced myself to think dispassionately, to see it from every side: who did I owe greatest allegiance to – my father or my mother? My father who sewed the seed, began me, or my mother who sheltered me inside her as I grew? My father then, I thought. Then there was the fact of her adultery: whatever grievance she had against my father, she should not have

debased herself and him by taking another man into her
bed, opening herself to another man, an impostor, a lesser
man, and when my father had gone to war to fight for all
our state.That Aigisthos had to die was clear to me. But
what of her? What of her? You say my actions have
undermined our civilisation, but I thought of civilisation,
of what was best for our people. I thought, the only true
deterrent is death. Another woman, here in the city, now,
who thought of murdering her husband must know that she
would pay with her life. Nothing less. Even then I lost my
nerve, swayed my own mind. For ten days I was going to
spare her, to stay away and not come back, abandon my
sister, deny my name. But the thought of my father raked
my soul. My father, my father, killed in cold blood, betrayed,
disposed of. And his breath was in my mouth and his tears
were in my eyes and I knew that he would find no peace
until he was avenged. The Gods. Apollo. I ran to Apollo's
temple. The Gods, the Gods, my only hope. I fell on my
knees and I begged for his help as though I were begging
for my life, because I was. And He came to me, He spoke
to me. The release of it. The hot, seeping release of it.
The decision was His, the orders were His: kill her and
Aigisthos too. Kill them. Avenge your father.

I came here, and I did it. The right thing. And it was well
done. For my God and for us all. It was well done.

TYNDAREOS. How dare you? How dare you try to soften me,
mollify me with your creeping, teary apology for yourself?

ORESTES. It is not an apology. / I am trying to explain. To
justify myself.

TYNDAREOS. Spewing forth your words, contrived words,
sure of their mark, full of contempt for those who hear
them. What is it to me that you thought about it long and
hard? Worse. Worse, in fact, that you did, that you had the
doubts, understood all the ways in which it was wrong, yet
still you couldn't stop your hand. What will be said of you,
as word of this atrocity spreads across the land, the world,
the whole of time? 'After much deliberation and thought,
and having asked the Gods' advice, Orestes killed his

mother'? No. They will say, 'Orestes killed his mother in cold blood, destroyed the name of a great house, dragged his sister into it, brought about their deaths and the destruction of a dynasty.'

ELECTRA. I wanted what he wanted. We did what we were told to do.

TYNDAREOS. Oh, I know you are not innocent, Electra. I saw your face as they closed your father's body in the tomb, the grey-stone expression in your eyes. I told you then, gently, with a gentle touch, to mourn out your anger in the proper fashion, to make your peace.

ELECTRA. A coward's way.

ORESTES. Don't Electra.

TYNDAREOS. You were always a watchful, untrustworthy child. I never liked you near me. But only now do I understand that you are full to your throat with recklessness.

MENELAOS. Enough now. Enough has been said.

ELECTRA. Not enough. Not enough. You listen to me now – /

ORESTES. Electra.

ELECTRA. We have listened to you, now you listen to me.

TYNDAREOS. Know your place and be silent.

ELECTRA. You are afraid to hear me. You are afraid to hear the truth.

TYNDAREOS. I fear nothing from you.

ELECTRA. You claim you are the great upholder of the law, you claim you are the champion of due process and restraint – /

TYNDAREOS. I do not claim so. It is so.

ELECTRA. And yet you cry for us to be thrown to the mob. You want to see us stoned, battered, torn limb from limb in some stinking alleyway.

TYNDAREOS. Because you are beyond the law. You put yourselves beyond the law.

ELECTRA. Then you be the one to bring the law to bear. You with your weight and your wisdom. You are are not a child alone and desperate as he was, as I was – /

TYNDAREOS. Oh, so you are children now.

ELECTRA. You be the one to break the chain of death on death. You be the one to stand before the assembly and demand that we be dealt with according to the law.

TYNDAREOS. Too late for that. The people are frantic for your blood.

ELECTRA. So your law is not so strong as you claim it is.

TYNDAREOS. How dare you?

ELECTRA. It is a light thing. It can be blown and bent by the breath of angry people.

TYNDAREOS. Your crime provokes beyond all reason.

ELECTRA. Why didn't you act against her and Aigisthos? The moment you knew what they had done? Where were you then? When you whispered to me at my father's funeral, urged me to silence, I thought you planned some retribution of your own. Justice. You, with the whole weight of the world behind you. But no. Weeks and weeks passed and you did nothing. The morning I was sent away to a shameful, degrading marriage, even then I looked for you but still you didn't come. And then the rumours reached me. I heard you went to dine with them, that you sat down and drank with them, flattered them, took gifts from them.

TYNDAREOS. Lies.

ELECTRA. And I realised, I realised it suited you, perhaps, to have a son-in-law in power, a son-in-law you could control, / in thrall to you.

TYNDAREOS. How dare you say so?

ELECTRA. It is the truth. You use the law when it suits you, you harness it, you hide behind it, modify it.

TYNDAREOS. Insolent wretch.

MENELAOS. Be silent now, Electra.

In another part of the palace the SLAVE *begins to sing to the baby.*

ELECTRA. Your absolute law does not exist. It is timing and advantage. It is power. It is money. It is greed. /

ORESTES. Oh, no. She is coming.

ELECTRA. Only the Gods can know true justice.

TYNDAREOS. You push me too far.

MENELAOS. Enough.

ORESTES. Leave me alone. Apollo, protect me.

ELECTRA. How many of the men who sit on your assembly do so with clean, transparent souls? One in a hundred? And you are not the one. You are not the one.

TYNDAREOS goes to strike ELECTRA. MENELAOS stops him.

MENELAOS. No.

TYNDAREOS. Get your hands off me. Off me.

ELECTRA goes to ORESTES, who is shaking and blocking his ears against the sound of the singing.

ORESTES. Let me be, I beg of you. My soul is gone already.

ELECTRA. Orestes.

ORESTES. Don't cry. Don't cry. What have I done to you?

ELECTRA. Stop it, please.

ORESTES. Stay away from me.

TYNDAREOS (*to* MENELAOS). You would side with them, would you? Fight for them? Are they your chosen ones? The future of your line?

The singing stops. Now, from outside the palace walls, the sound of a bell can be heard, ringing solemnly.

(*To* MENELAOS.) The assembly is convening. If you oppose me in this, I will break you.

MENELAOS. You dare to threaten me?

TYNDAREOS. I am more than one man.

MENELAOS. And I am Menelaos.

TYNDAREOS. Who is Menelaos? Who is this man who has been gone so long? I want to know. The people want to know. This city is desperate now for leadership. Your city. Your city, Menelaos.

(*To* ORESTES *and* ELECTRA.) Do you hear that? Murderers? That is the sound of your own death.

He leaves.

MENELAOS *watches* ORESTES *and* ELECTRA.

ELECTRA. He needs to eat. He needs to sleep. That's all. He needs so much to sleep.

MENELAOS. Where is Apollo? Why does He allow this if he has done His bidding?

ELECTRA. Apollo is here. He is watching us.

MENELAOS. Is He?

ELECTRA. You doubt Him?

MENELAOS. I only wonder why He has abandoned him.

ELECTRA. He has not abandoned us. He has brought us you.

She looks at him – challenging him.

Apollo didn't say it would be easy. Since when have the Gods made things easy for us? You know that. You of all people, married to *her*. What need would we of faith if everything were easy?

MENELAOS. You should learn to curb your tongue, Electra.

ELECTRA. For when? So I can die demurely? So I can die a silent death today?

MENELAOS *holds her gaze for a few moments but then looks away.* ORESTES *begins to recover.*

ORESTES. What happened?

ELECTRA. It's all right. You're all right now.

ORESTES. This terror. This affliction.

ELECTRA. It will pass.

ELECTRA *helps him to drink some water.*

ORESTES. Don't be alarmed, Uncle. I am myself again.

What are you thinking, Uncle?

MENELAOS. I am thinking.

ORESTES. They will be coming for us soon. There is very little time. Call your troops now. Surround the palace before it is too late.

Uncle? You will help us?

MENELAOS. Yes. Of course I must help you.

ORESTES. For our father's sake.

MENELAOS. Yes.

ORESTES. You have a child of your own now.

MENELAOS. Why do you say that?

ORESTES. Only because you must know now what it cost my father to sacrifice his child for you.

MENELAOS. I understood that then. With or without a child.

ORESTES. Not so much is being asked of you. Only that you save us. That you protect us now.

MENELAOS. I have no troops. I have a dozen men with me, that's all. Hardly enough to surround the palace. Not enough to defend it.

ORESTES. No troops?

MENELAOS. All my men are dead. Some in the earth. Some in the sea. Fallen away from me, one by one.

ORESTES. No troops.

MENELAOS. But even if they were all back with me, as they are in my dreams, I would not ask them to turn against the people.

ORESTES. You wouldn't have to. A show of strength from you and / they would back away.

MENELAOS. Force is not the answer here. It was never going to be.

ORESTES. There is no help then. We are lost.

MENELAOS. No. Listen to me now, Orestes: I will speak to them. I will go to the assembly and I will speak to them.

ORESTES. Speak to them? You will stand up and speak for us?

MENELAOS. I will identify leaders of factions, whisper quiet words in their ears, well-timed words. I will win them to you.

ORESTES. You can do that?

MENELAOS. Yes. You're very young and headstrong, it's hard for you to understand. They will bluster, argue, fight amongst themselves and then, when all is uproar and confusion, then my quiet words will start to tell and I will push home my advantage.

ORESTES. You can do that?

MENELAOS. Yes. Trust me in this. Trust me.

I should go now.

ORESTES. Yes. Or it will be too late.

MENELAOS. Will you be all right here?

ORESTES. Yes.

MENELAOS. I'll come back with news for you. Good news. You'll be all right, Electra?

She doesn't reply. MENELAOS *starts to go. He hesitates.*

I'll send more water for you. I'll send food.

ORESTES. Thank you.

MENELAOS. I think that would be best. Yes. I think this is best.

MENELAOS *leaves*.

ORESTES. Hope. Hope is like the sun. Simple I know, but it's true. The sun has come out inside me.

Come here.

He embraces ELECTRA.

We are not alone. We are not alone now.

When the water comes, let's wash. We'll wash away these tears, these frowns. And when we are clean, let's kneel and pray to Apollo. Lets give Him thanks. Ask Him to send our uncle all the strength he needs.

ELECTRA. He won't help us.

ORESTES. It will be hard, it's true. But he is a great man, long respected. The people do not forget a man like that. He is a legend.

ELECTRA. The kind of man they would want to lead them. The kind of man who could rule from this palace, with his wife and child beside him. Better than the matricides, the filthy children, the mad children.

ORESTES. What are you talking about?

ELECTRA. He won't help us. He doesn't want to help us.

ORESTES. No. No. No Electra. He will help us. He will do everything he can for us. It's hard for you to believe in him, I know. Hard for you to believe in anyone, you lived so long amongst dishonour and deceit.

ELECTRA. And learnt the way of things.

ORESTES. No. No. There are some good men, Electra. Good people. Men like our father, honourable to the end. The man I found you with – the peasant – you told me he was good. He never lied to you, did he? He kept his word to you.

When he swore he wouldn't touch you, did he ever break
his oath?

ELECTRA. No.

ORESTES. And the men that I grew up with, who raised me,
they weren't great men but they were good. Open, honest
men.

ELECTRA. Menelaos is not an open, honest man; Menelaos is
a politician.

ORESTES. He is a soldier. A hero. He is our father's brother,
made from the same stuff. He knows what duty is. What
honour is.

ELECTRA. He will go and speak to them, pretend to try, say a
few words to him or him, but when he meets with
opposition he will let himself be beaten down, ruefully,
politely, so as not to make enemies.

ORESTES. You're wrong. He will do the right thing. His
conscience will dictate that.

ELECTRA. His conscience? I'm not sure that his conscience
will trouble him too much. A man who took the whole city
to war for the sake of his pride, who took away a generation
and came back with twelve men. A man like that must keep
his conscience at his heel like a well-trained dog.

ORESTES. Stop it.

He moves away from her.

ELECTRA. I'm sorry. I don't want to be the one to crush your
hopes. But you have to know. You have to see. I want you to
be ready. We were ready before. Before he came. We can be
ready again. Orestes. Please believe what I say.

He turns to her.

ORESTES. Everything is going to be all right. Everything.
Dear, dear Electra. You have cared for me, helped me.

ELECTRA. And I will always do so.

ORESTES. I couldn't have asked for a nurse more gentle, a braver nurse. But now I am going to care for you. And everything will be all right.

I will go to the assembly myself.

ELECTRA. What?

ORESTES. I will watch Menelaos, listen to him, and when the time is right, I will help him. I don't know why I didn't think of it before.

ELECTRA. You can't go.

ORESTES. Why should he have to speak for us? It's our fate they are deciding. I am a man. I'll show them that.

ELECTRA. You can't go.

ORESTES. I'm not the cringing, broken boy they've heard about. I am Agamemnon's son.

ELECTRA. If you leave here now they will attack you on the streets.

ORESTES. No. No one will dare to harm me until the sentence has been passed. They are law abiding people, I can depend on that. And even the most unruly amongst them would hesitate to touch me now that Menelaos is back.

ELECTRA. You can't go. I won't let you go.

ORESTES. What have I to lose?

ELECTRA. They'll hurt you. / They'll take you away from me.

ORESTES. If I can help Menelaos in any way I can, then I must do it.

ELECTRA. They'll take you away.

ORESTES. Surely you must see that?

ELECTRA. What if I am right? What if he doesn't mean to help us?

ORESTES. You're not right.

ELECTRA. I'm coming with you then.

ORESTES. No.

ELECTRA. Yes.

ORESTES. No. It's safer for you here.

ELECTRA. What if you need me? You're not well. What if the madness comes again?

ORESTES. It won't. Because I'm not afraid anymore. I'm not alone anymore.

ELECTRA. You never were alone.

ORESTES. No. I know. I didn't / mean that.

ELECTRA. I'll come with you and we'll stand together. We'll show them we're together in this / and in everything.

ORESTES. No. They wouldn't let you into the assembly. If you tried to speak it would be seen as contempt. We can't infuriate them.

ELECTRA. So that's what I am now. Your liability. That's it now. The ludicrous female who threatens to make you blush in front of your peers. You are a man now and what am I? What am I?

Sorry. I'm sorry. I'm so sorry.

ORESTES. Electra, it will be almost over. Give this to me, please. Please. Stay here and wait for me.

ELECTRA. I can't.

ORESTES. You can.

ELECTRA. No.

ORESTES. And I will come back. Very soon. With Menelaos. And everything will be all right.

ELECTRA. Please don't do this.

ORESTES. This is not the last day. Yes?

ELECTRA. Yes.

He leaves. ELECTRA *listens to the door closing. After a
few moments she rushes to the door as if she would follow
him. But she stops herself.*

I was not born right.

Where is my woman's patience? Where is that benignity
that's meant to be inside me, that's meant to ease these
waiting, waiting torments?

Don't leave me here.

Or do they learn it, my clever sisters, is there some trick,
some knack, some anaesthetic of the heart that no one ever
taught to me? Wait here Electra, wait here Electra. Wait for
your father, wait for your lover, wait for your brother. I will
go mad.

Orestes.

What will I do if he doesn't come back?

What if he is dead already?

What if he was wrong and they set upon him, tear him
down before he has a chance to speak? There are some
hard-edged men in that assembly, supporters of Aigisthos
who wanted him to rule, with my mother as his puppet
consort – men who came to dine here late at night, who
drank and looked me up and down, they would not hesitate
to kill him on the spot, revenge for their friend, the chance
of power for any one of them.

What if he is dead?

What if they leave me waiting here? What if they make me
die alone? What if they make me live, go on living year after
year, a shamed life, a barren life, waiting for death? Waiting.
I want Orestes. I want my brother. I want him with me.

I am too like my mother. I am all my mother and none of
my father. It is her blood, her blood that rages in my veins.

(*To the mirror.*) Look at us. Your hot, triumphant eyes
staring back at me. May the Gods damn you for what
you've done to me.

The SLAVE *enters. She is holding the baby and has brought some food and water. She places it down.*

Thank you.

SLAVE. You are welcome.

The SLAVE *starts to go.*

ELECTRA. Wait. Are you afraid of me?

SLAVE. I am afraid of no one. I fear only the Gods.

ELECTRA. They make you serve and yet you do it gently, graciously – how do you do that?

SLAVE. All of us are humble servants. Nothing more.

ELECTRA. They make you serve and yet you sing. I have heard you.

SLAVE. I was taught to take my pain and make a thing of beauty. My song frees my soul. It takes me back to my country, to my family, to each child they made me leave behind.

ELECTRA. The baby – they make you feed her when you must hate her and wish it was your own child in your arms. You must want to kill her, even as she sucks, fill her mouth too full with milk, suffocate her in the night, drop her, trample her. Tell me that you feel those things.

SLAVE. I love her, this child. I love her because she is not mine. The Gods say it is the way to peace – to love what is not mine.

ELECTRA. Your Gods must be very different from mine.

SLAVE. Your Gods and my Gods, they are the same. We share the same Gods, you and I.

She starts to leave again.

ELECTRA. Wait. Stay with me. Please. I like to have you with me. May I see the baby?

The SLAVE *allows her to see.*

Hermione. My twice cousin. Almost my sister. Treasured child. Lucky child.

I have no children. Nor ever will have, I suppose. But then she must have told you that – your mistress. Laughed at my virginity. Untouched . . .

Sing to me. Sing to me and I will try to pray.

The SLAVE *sings.* ELECTRA *kneels and prays. After a few minutes the sound of the ringing bell can be heard.* ELECTRA *finishes her prayer.*

It's over. Go and look, please. I can't bear to. Watch for my brother. Tell me if he is coming back.

The SLAVE *goes out of the door.*

Apollo, great Apollo, don't desert me, I beg of you. Bring him back to me, I beg of you. I beg of you.

What's that noise? People.

The SLAVE *returns.*

Is he there? What's happening? Tell me.

SLAVE. Your brother is coming.

ELECTRA. He's coming?

The SLAVE *nods.*

Alive? Is he alive? Walking?

SLAVE. Yes.

ELECTRA. Thank you. Thank you. You are certain it is him?

SLAVE. Your brother is coming. In his hands he holds two knives.

ELECTRA. Knives?

SLAVE. There are many people with him. They are weeping, moaning. They tear their hair.

ELECTRA. Is Menelaos with him? Your master?

ORESTES *enters. He is holding two knives.*

ORESTES (*to* SLAVE). Get out of here.

> SLAVE *starts to go.*

No, wait. Where is your master?

SLAVE. I don't / know, Sir.

ORESTES. Is he here in the palace?

SLAVE. No, Sir. I don't / know, Sir.

ORESTES. Is he hiding? Hiding under a bed? Crouching behind a chair like the coward that he is?

> *The baby starts to cry.*

SLAVE. I don't know, Sir, where he is. I stay with my mistress.

ORESTES. Your mistress? Where is she?

SLAVE. In her rooms, Sir.

ORESTES. Doing what?

SLAVE. I don't know, Sir.

ORESTES. Was she anxious? Did she seem afraid?

SLAVE. No, Sir. She is happy today. She is smiling.

ORESTES. Smiling. She is smiling.

> Leave us. Go.

> *The* SLAVE *leaves.*

> Two knives, Electra. One for me and one for you.

> *She stares at them.*

ELECTRA. Two knives.

ORESTES. We kill ourselves within the hour or they will come for us and they will take us out and stone us.

ELECTRA. Menelaos?

ORESTES. Didn't come. You were right and you were wrong: he didn't even pretend to try.

> No Menelaos. No justice. No help.

ELECTRA. Within the hour.

ORESTES. It was all but finished before I arrived. The decision almost made. A few last men were shouting against us, seizing their share of vitriolic glory. I did hear one man speak for us, a grey haired man with the wisest eyes who said they should all think of Agamemnon first, and what was done was done for him. He said we should be banished. Nothing more. But a hundred voices came back at him, all chanting 'stone them, stone them', and our grandfather chief amongst them, livid and red-faced, springing to his feet, his arm raised in the air. I stepped out before them and I spoke. They recoiled in horror, gawped at me as though I was already dead. But I was not afraid of them. I used the anger that had risen up inside me, my anger with Menelaos. I cried out that we had done Apollo's will, that they should take their outrage and lay it at His feet. But they shouted me down, they drowned my words. A stone hit me hard on the head – here. But I did not buckle. I stood firm.

ELECTRA. How brave you were.

ORESTES. They saw that I was a man and some little fear, some respect crept into their minds. I won for us the chance to end our lives ourselves.

ELECTRA. You touched their hearts, Orestes.

ORESTES. I don't want their sympathy. I don't want their scratched faces, their tears. What do I want with their sympathy? I want justice.

The treacherous, unnatural coward. Not even the guts to tell me. He couldn't even face me. He lied. He lied to me. We are his family. He owes us. He owes my father. He owes us. He could have swayed them. I know he could. Those men in there weren't leaders; strong-mouthed but not strong-minded, all of them. He could have made them see. We would have been banished, sent to some island temple to cleanse our souls and make amends. Two years, three years away and then we could have come back here and ruled as we were meant to rule. But that will never happen now. That will never be. It is now that we die because of him.

He forces the knife into her hand.

Take it. Take it up. Come on. Will you cut me first, or will I cut you? Take it. Let's do it now and give them what they want, spill our cursed blood onto the ground. Take it.

ELECTRA *begins to cry.* ORESTES *is silent for a few moments.*

I have failed you.

ELECTRA. No. A sudden sadness, that is all. That it should end like this.

It's gone. I've lost it – my bright vision of our perfect death. It is dirty. Dirty and ugly. Ugly and pathetic. Where was I? How was I seeing? Whose eyes were those? Not mine. Not mine.

ORESTES. Stop.

ELECTRA. I can't remember how I felt so reconciled.

I'm sorry. I'm so sorry.

ORESTES. I have taken everything from you.

ELECTRA. There was nothing to take.

ORESTES. I should never have come to you. I should have killed her and then killed myself and let that be an end.

ELECTRA. No. No. No. My only joy has been your coming. My only joy.

ORESTES. What is it you said to me? What is it we have to hold to? We will be rocked in Apollo's arms. We will be all satisfaction.

ELECTRA. In a place where there is gentleness and light.

ORESTES. And it will be so. I promise you. It will be so.

ELECTRA. How can it be? How can there be peace when there is so much anger in our hearts?

ORESTES. It will be so. They will not take this from us. You and I. There is nothing else.

Let's do it well, Electra.

ELECTRA. Yes. Let's do it well.

ORESTES. Like the children of a King.

ELECTRA. Yes.

ORESTES. Let me clean your face.

He cleans away the blood and dirt. She does the same for him. They smile.

They will come in here and think to find the bodies of two murderers, wretched, coiled upon the ground, the fear rigid on our faces.

ELECTRA. But we will show them who we are.

ORESTES. Lie still and calm and hand in hand.

ELECTRA. Our goodness arrayed around our heads like the light of a God.

ORESTES. A sculpture. A shrine.

He throws open cupboards and pulls out clothes.

Clothes for princes. For princes and princesses. No King had greater riches in his tomb.

ELECTRA. And we'll sit and eat.

She goes to the bed and lays out food.

And stories will be told of our last breakfast and how we drank and smiled before we died.

ORESTES *has put on a golden cloak. She looks at him.*

That cloak. My father sent for us, asked us to bring Iphegenia to the coast, to her wedding – so we thought. My mother wore that cloak. She said it would reflect the sun, set alight my father's heart and he would soon be gone to war. Make him remember her. You were there.

ORESTES. Was I?

ELECTRA. A babe in arms. I held you in the carriage when you cried. We sang to you. All of us. My mother too.

ORESTES. A family.

ELECTRA. Yes.

ORESTES. She did love my father, didn't she?

ELECTRA. Yes. Or nothing in the world is true. She loved my father. She loved you. She loved my sisters.

ORESTES. And she loved you.

He hands her a dress.

Wear this.

She undresses and puts on the dress.

My beautiful sister.

ELECTRA *goes to the dressing table and looks at herself in the mirror. She reaches out and touches the glass. She picks up a bottle of perfume and puts some on her throat.*

She picks up the brush and brushes her hair. ORESTES *watches her.*

When she has finished she walks over to the bed and sits down. He goes to sit with her. They eat.

It was my favourite thing, when I was very young, to sit and eat beneath the trees, when a summer's day was done. All of us together, my guardians, my friends, sitting beneath the orange trees, within the whisper of the sea, feasting until the sun went down. And I could ask my questions then. Everything which puzzled me. And they'd try to give me answers, through the wine. To explain why men were always fighting, and why the Gods were loath to intervene, and what makes a king a great king, and why we have to die. And they'd laugh at me, call me the questioning boy, call me serious and keen. And on those nights I wouldn't sleep. I'd go and lie where I could see the stars, and throb and pulse with the sense of who I was and all the possibilities of me.

I felt, I think, how a God must feel.

I only ever wanted to be good. To be worthy of my father's name. A good king. Remembered well. No one will ever know that now.

ELECTRA. Apollo will know. I will know.

He is staring at her.

ORESTES. I can't hurt you, Electra. Don't ask me to.

ELECTRA. And I can't hurt you.

ORESTES. We must see to ourselves then.

ELECTRA. Yes.

ORESTES. In the same moment. The same second.

ELECTRA. I've never held a knife – not one so sharp.

ORESTES. Be sure to place it here.

He touches her heart.

ELECTRA. Will you hold me, Orestes?

He takes her in his arms.

The only arms I'll ever know.

They begin to kiss.

Let this kiss be every kiss. Every bed, every night, every
child I would have had. My life. My life in your arms.

They kiss passionately.

Orestes.

They stop kissing. They are trembling. ORESTES *stares into
her eyes.*

ORESTES. Why should we die? No. No. I won't do it.

ELECTRA. What do you mean?

ORESTES. I won't do it. Why should we die?

ELECTRA. Orestes.

ORESTES. Why should we die?

ELECTRA. What choice do we have? / No choice.

ORESTES. Why should we die? When he will bring her to this
bed, our bed, when he will lie her down and love her, go on

loving, living, ruling, taking everything we should have had, when he betrayed us?

ELECTRA. Orestes. Please.

ORESTES. Why should we die?

ELECTRA. Don't think about them. Don't think / about what happens afterwards.

ORESTES. Yes, think about them. Think about them. He will live and breathe when we are gone. He will / take it all.

ELECTRA. He won't know happiness. A man like that, dead in his heart / it is a hollow victory.

ORESTES. Happiness? Every time he touches her, every time his child touches his face he will know happiness. Every time the people bow down at his feet.

We have done nothing wrong. Did we do wrong?

ELECTRA. No.

ORESTES. We did what Apollo commanded us to do, while he and that whore Helen asked the deaths of thousands upon thousands of men, killed fathers, husbands, brothers, sons, destroyed lives, and for what? Nothing so great as a father's honour. Nothing so great as that.

ELECTRA. She was the cause of everything, it's true. It was for her my father took our sister's life, for her my mother killed him, for her we killed our mother too.

ORESTES. She's up there now, in her room and she is smiling. This is a happy day for her.

ELECTRA. She will be making lists of what she will and will not keep, going through my father's things, labelling, discarding as though we are already dead.

ORESTES. And when he comes she'll walk in here with him. They'll find our bodies and throw them on the pyre and know that everything is theirs and it is over. It is my life. And your life. I cannot make my peace with this.

ELECTRA. Let's kill her then.

ORESTES. Kill her?

ELECTRA. Let's take her with us.

Let's break his heart.

Let's wreck his victory.

Let's finish her.

ORESTES. Kill her?

ELECTRA. The Gods would be pleased, I'm certain, to see the end of Zeus's monstrous creation. And the people too would love us then. They will love us, won't they? No more 'matricides'. We'll be the heroes who rid them of a curse, a scourge, the mistress of lust and vanity, the shame of all her sex.

This is why Apollo brought them back. Not so Menelaos could save us but so that we can do this thing, this service to the earth. Our gift before we die.

ORESTES. You are more than a woman. You are a man too. You are the bravest, strongest creature I have ever known. We do it then.

ELECTRA. Yes.

ORESTES. How?

ELECTRA. We'll go to her, our knives concealed. Look broken, suppliant. We'll ask if we can speak to her alone. We'll tell her we're about to die, fall on our knees and cry, beg her forgiveness for everything we've done. And when her guard is down and she is all condescension and concern, well then . . .

ORESTES. Then I will run her through.

ELECTRA. She won't expect it. She is so arrogant, so vain, she'd never believe we would dare to strike.

ORESTES. Who will be with her?

ELECTRA. Only her women. I can keep them back with this.

ORESTES. And what if there are soldiers there? Menelaos' men?

ELECTRA. Well, then we will die fighting. They will do our job for us.

ORESTES. There will be blood. There will be more blood.

ELECTRA. Poison. Not blood. It is poison in her veins. Be glad to see it flow.

ORESTES. Does she look like my mother?

ELECTRA. No.

No.

ORESTES. There is no time left.

Let's pray together.

They kneel beside each other.

Great Apollo, you have been my guide in everything I've done. You filled me with your power, with your certainty when I was most in need. Do not forsake me now. Give me the strength to do your work once more. Receive me into your everlasting light.

ELECTRA. My Father, if you can hear your daughter's prayer, send us your blessing. We kill for you, we die for you. Give us your courage. Help your loyal children now.

ORESTES. In Apollo's name we pray.

ELECTRA. In our God we place our trust.

They stop praying and look at each other.

ORESTES. It is now, then.

ELECTRA. Love me, Orestes.

ORESTES. I love you.

They go out of the door.

A few moments later, MENELAOS *enters. His sword is drawn. He is escorted by a* SOLDIER. *He stops in the doorway.*

MENELAOS (*to* SOLDIER). Wait there. This sight should meet my eyes alone.

He looks about the room. Searches.

Not here. Where else would they have gone? A place to die in? Surely they would not have dared delay. They would not be so stupid, surely.

The SLAVE *comes rushing towards the door.*

SLAVE. Help me. Help me.

The SOLDIER *grabs hold of her and restrains her.*

MENELAOS. Leave her.

(*To* SLAVE.) What has happened? Speak to me.

SLAVE. I didn't want to let her go. I tried to hold her but there was the knife. They held it here. They pulled her from my arms.

MENELAOS. What are you talking about?

SLAVE. The baby. They have taken the baby. I tried. / I didn't want to let her go.

MENELAOS. Who have? Who have?

SLAVE. Electra. Her brother. They have taken the baby. Hermione.

MENELAOS *hits her hard. She falls to the ground.*

MENELAOS. Where are they? Where is Helen?

SLAVE. Oh, no. Oh, no. Oh, no.

MENELAOS. Where is my wife?

SLAVE. Dead. She is dead.

MENELAOS. Dead?

SLAVE. They killed her. They came into her room, crying. They asked if they could speak to her alone. She told us to leave her. All her women. She was certain. Loud. And so we left. And then we heard her scream. And we ran back to her, but he was killing her, striking her. She wasn't dying. There was blood. She was crying out for you, crying out your

name. He struck her harder, harder, harder until she fell.
Her life was gone.

MENELAOS. No. No.

SLAVE. There was screaming. Her women. Some running
from the room. I ran to her, my legs were slow. He roared.
An animal. He fell onto his knees. Weeping loud. And
Electra, the girl, shouting always shouting. She saw me
then. She saw the baby. She pushed the knife against my
flesh. He came to me. Eyes white. Mad. Tears and blood.
He pulled the baby from my hands, pulled back my fingers
one by one.

MENELAOS. They will die for this. Where are they? Where
have they taken her?

SLAVE. I don't know. I don't know, Sir.

MENELAOS. Orestes.

Fire can be seen coming from another part of the palace.

SLAVE. Fire.

MENELAOS. Fire. The Gods protect her.

(*To* SOLDIER.) Sound the alarm. They are not dead. The
matricides. Fire in the palace. Sound the alarm.

The SOLDIER *rushes away.*

MENELAOS *moves towards the door, but is stopped by the
sight of* ORESTES *and* ELECTRA. *They have stepped out
onto a balcony (or roof), high above.* ORESTES *is holding*
HERMIONE. *He and* ELECTRA *are splattered with blood.*

Give her back, Orestes. Give me my child.

ELECTRA. Give us our lives and we will give you your child.

MENELAOS. You give me my child. Now.

ORESTES. This child? But you owe me this child. You owed
this child to my father and now you owe her to me.

MENELAOS. If you hurt her I will kill you.

ORESTES. But you are not good at remembering what you owe. Are you? You're not good at paying your debts. Menelaos? Uncle?

MENELAOS. Give her to me.

ORESTES. You didn't come. You didn't come. You / didn't come.

MENELAOS. What do you want, Orestes?

ORESTES. 'Trust me. Trust me, Orestes.'

MENELAOS. What do you want?

ORESTES. I want you gone. That's what I want. Out of this city. I want you gone. I am the King.

From outside the palace, alarm bells begin to ring.

MENELAOS. You? A King?

ELECTRA. Don't argue with us, Menelaos.

MENELAOS. You are mad. You are insane. You think the people will follow you? A matricide – spitting blood with every word you speak? You have murdered my wife. Murderer. Was it good, Orestes, to feel a woman's flesh against your blade again?

ORESTES. Helen? Helen? No. Helen is not dead. When I tried to kill her . . . I did try, but the Gods came down and took her away. One of their own.

MENELAOS. What lies are these?

ORESTES. Set her in the heavens. A new star in the sky.

MENELAOS (*to* SLAVE). Is this true? Did you see this too?

SLAVE. She is dead. I swear she is dead.

MENELAOS. I loved her. I gave my life to her.

ORESTES. The sky opened. A great white light. The roof split. Almighty Zeus reached down. He picked her up with one hand. I saw it. Electra saw it too.

SOLDIERS *appear in the doorway behind* MENELAOS.
Flames are rising behind ORESTES.

ELECTRA. Just let us go, Menelaos.

MENELAOS. You are dripping in her blood.

ORESTES. Apollo. Apollo. Come to me now.

ELECTRA. Let us go. Take us to the border and you will have
the baby.

MENELAOS. You will never walk away from here alive. The
palace is surrounded. You will pay for what you've done.

ORESTES. Then she will pay. She will pay for what you've
done. If our blood is cursed then so is hers. If we must die
then so must she. The end of Helen's line.

He holds the baby out as though he will drop her.

MENELAOS. Stop.

ELECTRA. No. No, Orestes. No. Menelaos, let us go. Just let
us go. Somewhere quiet where I can take care of him /
make him well.

MENELAOS. Give me the child. Bring her to me. I'll let you
go.

ELECTRA. The flames. The flames are high.

MENELAOS. Give me my child.

HELEN*'s dead body is carried in by a* SOLDIER.

No. No. See what you have done.

ORESTES *looks at the body but will not see it.*

ORESTES. Apollo is coming. He is coming. Do you see,
Electra? The light is here.

ELECTRA. Keep calm, Orestes. Look at me.

MENELAOS. Do you want more blood on your hands,
Electra?

ORESTES. Apollo, take me now. Take me to you.

ELECTRA. Orestes. Come to me. Orestes.

He steps onto the very edge of the drop.

ORESTES. Sit me by your side. In the light.

MENELAOS. Stop him.

ELECTRA. Orestes. Come to me.

MENELAOS. Don't hurt her. Please.

ELECTRA. Orestes. Orestes.

ORESTES. It would be good, to leave this world.

He steps off the edge. The baby is still in his arms.

ELECTRA. No.

For one moment, he is suspended in the air, in light.

ORESTES. Look. I am a God.

Darkness.

End.